A Day that Changed History

The Assassination of John F. Kennedy

Turning Points in History

TRACEY KELLY

A+

Smart Apple Media

First published in 2014 by Smart Apple Media
Smart Apple Media is an imprint of Black Rabbit Books

Smart Apple Media
P.O. Box 3263
Mankato, Minnesota 56002

Library of Congress Cataloging-in-Publication Data

Kelly, Tracey.
A day that changed history : the assassination of John F. Kennedy
/ Tracey Kelly.
    pages cm -- (Turning points in history)
Includes bibliographical references and index.
Summary: "Describes the life, accomplishments, and assassination
of John F. Kennedy"--Provided by publisher.

ISBN 978-1-59920-971-5 (library binding)

1. Kennedy, John F. (John Fitzgerald),
    1917-1963--Assassination- -Juvenile literature.
2. Kennedy, John F. (John Fitzgerald),
    1917-1963--Juvenile literature.
3. United States--History--1961-1969--Juvenile literature.
I. Title.
E842.9.K455 2013
973.922092--dc23
[B]

                                        2013003428

Editor: Sarah Ridley
Editor in Chief: John C. Miles
Designer: Jason Billin
Art director: Peter Scoulding
Picture research: Diana Morris

Picture credits: AFP/Getty Images: 33. AP/PAI: 12. Bettmann/
Corbis: front cover, 13, 30, 31, 34, 37, 38. Boston Globe/John
F. Kennedy Presidential Library & Museum, Boston: 8. Bill Clark/
Roll Call/Getty Images: 44. Bill Eppridge/Time & Life Pictures/
Getty Images: 41. Toni Frissell Collection, LOC/John F. Kennedy
Presidential Library & Museum, Boston: 14. The Granger Collectio
Topfoto: 5. Harper & Brothers, New York, 1956: 17 inset. Bob
Jackson/AP/PAI: 39. John F. Kennedy Library Foundation: 9. John
F. Kennedy Presidential Library & Museum, Boston: 10, 18. Robe
Knudsen, White House Photographs/John F. Kennedy Presidential
Library & Museum, Boston: 15, 27. LOC, Washington DC: 28. Ca
Mydans/Time & Life Pictures/Getty Images: 16. NASA: 24, 43.
Hy Pesking for Look Magazine, LOC/John F. Kennedy Presidential
Library & Museum, Boston: 7. Pictorial Parade/Getty Images: 19.
Rex Features: 45. Rolls Press/Popperfoto/Getty Images: 22. Abbie
Rowe, National Park Service/John F. Kennedy Presidential Library
Museum, Boston: 32, 36, 40. Paul Schutzer, Time & Life Pictures
Getty Images: 21. Richard Sears/John F. Kennedy Presidential
Library & Museum, Boston: 6. Cecil Stoughton, White House
Photographs/John F. Kennedy Presidential Library & Museum,
Boston: 4, 23, 25, 35. Touchstone Books : 42. U.S. Army Signal
Corps/John F. Kennedy Presidential Library & Museum, Boston: 2
U.S. Navy: 11. U.S. News World Report Magazine Collection, LOC
Washington DC: 29. John Vachon for Look Magazine, LOC, /John
Kennedy Presidential Library & Museum, Boston: 17. World Histo
Archive/Topfoto: 26.

Printed in the United States of America at
Corporate Graphics, North Mankato, Minnesota.

PO 1651
3-2014

9 8 7 6 5 4 3

CONTENTS

The Kennedy family:
(left to right) Caroline,
John F. Kennedy,
Jackie, and John Jr.

John Fitzgerald Kennedy was one of the most influential and best-loved leaders in 20th century history. But even before he took up his post as 35th President of the United States in 1961, John F. Kennedy (JFK) had made his mark as a U.S. Navy Lieutenant, war hero, award-winning writer, congressman, and senator. Kennedy's privileged background gave him the means to study and make the most of his natural talents. His large and affectionate family helped to launch and support his political career after World War II. But perhaps his most important advantage was his inborn idealism and humanitarianism: he wanted to make America a fairer and more prosperous place for all its citizens, regardless of heritage, religion, or class.

This book provides a timeline in pictures and words of JFK's brief yet remarkable life. It tells the story of his childhood, early career, work as president, tragic assassination, and its aftermath. But it also tells the story of the amazing legacy he left for future generations. His work in the White House included strengthening civil rights, establishing organizations such as the Peace Corps, and launching NASA's Apollo program. Within his own family, JFK inspired his brothers, Robert and Edward, to follow in his political footsteps, as well as inspiring two future presidents–Bill Clinton and Barack Obama.

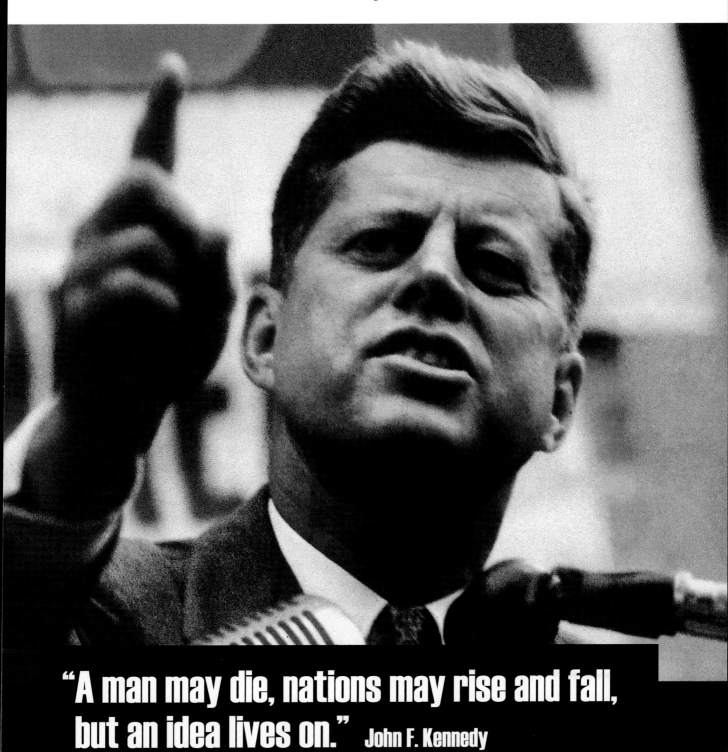

"A man may die, nations may rise and fall, but an idea lives on." John F. Kennedy

John (back row, left) and his large family spent many happy summers at their vacation home on Cape Cod.

Born on May 29, 1917, in Brookline, Massachusetts, John Fitzgerald Kennedy was the second eldest of nine children. His mother Rose Fitzgerald was the daughter of a Boston mayor; his father Joseph Kennedy, Sr. was a successful businessman who had made a large fortune. John (or "Jack" as he was called) and his siblings enjoyed a very comfortable upbringing, living in a large house with servants in Boston. Summers were spent by the sea in nearby Hyannis Port, on Cape Cod. The Kennedys belonged to the Roman Catholic Church and were of Irish heritage. John was a sickly child, suffering from many childhood illnesses. As a young boy, he contracted life-threatening scarlet fever. His father visited him in the hospital every day for a month, terrified he would die. But Jack made it through this crisis, as he would make it through many others in the years to come.

At age14, Jack attended Choate, a boarding school for boys in Connecticut, where he played tennis, basketball, and football. He excelled at history and English but didn't do so well with other subjects, causing his father to write him a letter urging him to do better at schoolwork. However, Jack's sharp mind and individualist spirit were evident. His classmates were amazed that he had a daily subscription to *The New York Times*. A popular student, Jack was intelligent, attractive, funny, and charming–all ingredients that would help persuade people to vote for him later, when he entered politics.

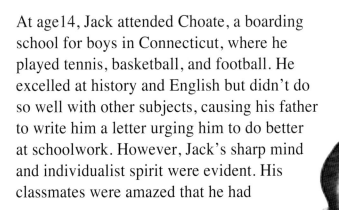

Jack with his father (top) and grandfather

"I will not be disappointed if you don't turn out to be a real genius, but I think you can be a really worthwhile citizen with good judgment and understanding." Joseph Kennedy, Sr.

Jack Kennedy studying in his room at Harvard University

Jack Kennedy's efforts to be a better pupil paid off, for he was accepted at the prestigious Princeton University in 1936, soon transferring to Harvard University where his brother Joseph already studied. At Harvard, Jack took history and government classes, but his grades were only average. Jack's political opinions began to develop and he became active in student groups. In the summer of 1937, he spent time traveling around Europe with a friend, which sparked his interest in foreign affairs. His father became U.S. Ambassador to the United Kingdom in 1938, so Jack returned to Europe, this time spending the summer working for the American Embassy in London.

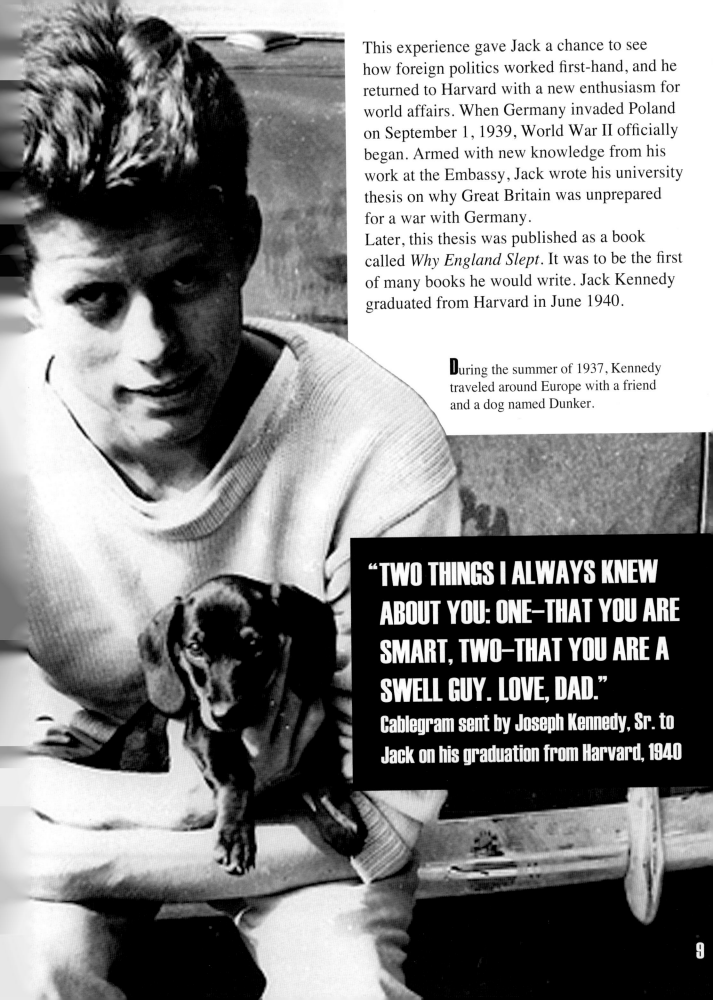

This experience gave Jack a chance to see how foreign politics worked first-hand, and he returned to Harvard with a new enthusiasm for world affairs. When Germany invaded Poland on September 1, 1939, World War II officially began. Armed with new knowledge from his work at the Embassy, Jack wrote his university thesis on why Great Britain was unprepared for a war with Germany.

Later, this thesis was published as a book called *Why England Slept*. It was to be the first of many books he would write. Jack Kennedy graduated from Harvard in June 1940.

During the summer of 1937, Kennedy traveled around Europe with a friend and a dog named Dunker.

"TWO THINGS I ALWAYS KNEW ABOUT YOU: ONE—THAT YOU ARE SMART, TWO—THAT YOU ARE A SWELL GUY. LOVE, DAD."

Cablegram sent by Joseph Kennedy, Sr. to Jack on his graduation from Harvard, 1940

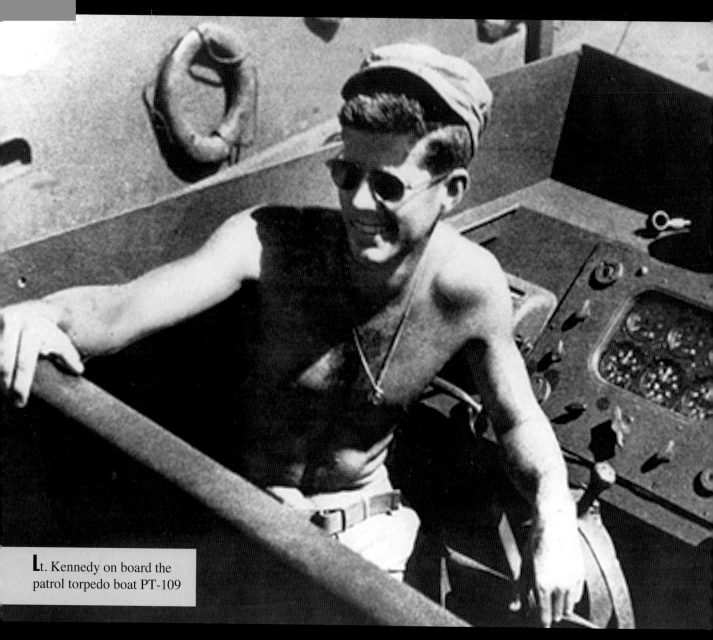

Lt. Kennedy on board the patrol torpedo boat PT-109

In October 1941, the world was deep in the throes of World War II. Jack Kennedy enlisted in the U.S. Navy, as did his brother Joe, who became a pilot. Jack was made Lieutenant (Lt.) and commander of a patrol torpedo boat, the PT-109. With a crew of 12 men, Lt. Kennedy was sent to the South Pacific. His job was to prevent Japanese boats

also to look for enemy ships to sink. On the night of August 2, 1943, the PT-109 was surprised by a Japanese destroyer, which rammed into it, splitting the boat in two. The collision caused a huge fire, and the boat eventually sank. Two men died, but the others managed to escape. The survivors clung to the wreckage overnight and then swam to an

Crew member Patrick McMahon was so badly burnt that he was unable to swim. Jack saved his life by clenching McMahon's life-jacket strap between his teeth, dragging him as he swam over 4 miles (6.5 km) to the nearest land. Once safely on the small island, the next step was to find food and organize a rescue. After several days, native islanders spotted the men; Jack carved an SOS message onto a piece of coconut shell and gave it to them so they could summon help. The PT-109 crew were rescued the next day. For his acts of leadership and bravery, Lt. Kennedy received the Purple Heart and the Navy Marine Corps medals in 1944. Sadly, his brother Joe Kennedy died the same year when his plane was blown up over Europe.

Jack Kennedy receives medals for his bravery and leadership, 1944.

and Purple Hearts

Jack reads what the press has to say about his campaign.

"The New Generation Offers a Leader."
John F. Kennedy campaign slogan, 1946

When Joe Kennedy, Jr. was young, he used to boast that someday he would become America's first Catholic president. Now that Joe was dead, the attention turned to brother Jack, who had originally wanted to be a teacher or writer. Joseph Kennedy, Sr. had a serious talk with Jack and convinced his son to run for congress as a Democrat.

Joseph Kennedy threw a huge amount of money into his son's campaign, about $250,000, and hired a public relations firm to manage Jack's image. As someone from a wealthy background, Jack campaigned hard to win working-class voters, visiting local organizations, chatting to people in the streets, and emphasizing his war record.

On November 4, 1946, at only 29 years old, John F. Kennedy became congressman of the Massachusetts eleventh congressional district–the post held by his grandfather, after whom he had been named. He was re-elected twice. During six years (three terms) in the U.S. House of Representatives, he voted for social welfare programs and was pro-union. Now with higher political ambitions, Congressman Kennedy decided to run for senator.

He campaigned all through 1952 against his Republican opponent, Henry Cabot Lodge Jr. with Joe Kennedy, Sr. again managing his campaign, but his overbearing manner upset people. So Robert (Bobby) Kennedy – Jack's younger brother–stepped in to become his campaign manager. It was a partnership that would last throughout his career. John F. Kennedy was elected senator for Massachusetts on November 4, 1952. He was sprinting up the political ladder.

JFK wades his way through a crowd of confetti-throwing well-wishers after victory in the 1952 U.S. Senate election.

Massachusetts Congressman to U.S. Senator

Jackie and Jack's marriage, 1953

As his career continued to prosper, Jack Kennedy's personal life also flourished. He met photojournalist Jacqueline Lee Bouvier at a dinner party in 1951, and they dated for two years. Like Jack, Jackie was from a wealthy, well-connected New England family, and also like Jack, she was intelligent, attractive, and charming. Born on June 28, 1929, Jackie was 12 years younger and had studied art, history, literature, and French in college. She had studied in Paris for a year, which she later wrote she "loved more than any other year of my life."

On September 12, 1953, Jackie Bouvier married Jack Kennedy at St. Mary's Church in Newport, Rhode Island. It was a union not only of two people but of two powerful American families.

In 1961, Jackie Kennedy would become a gracious First Lady who took her duties very seriously. She felt the White House was an important symbol of America's heritage and made it her mission to restore the 18th-century building, furnishing it with antiques and art from America's past. She even made a television documentary about it, watched by 80 million people.

Mrs. Kennedy became a figurehead for charities and a goodwill ambassador, traveling to Pakistan, Greece, Austria, and France, but she felt her first job was to support her husband and to be a great mother. She turned the sun porch into a kindergarten for their children Caroline (1957-) and John Jr. (1960-1999). Jackie also became a style icon for women across the United States.

Jackie Kennedy accepts an antique jug in the newly renovated White House.

"If you bungle raising your children, I don't think whatever else you do matters very much."
Jacqueline Bouvier Kennedy

Marriage to Jacqueline Bouvier–First Lady

Despite multiple health issues, JFK was an energetic campaigner.

Problems caused by a back injury he had suffered during World War II caused him so much pain that on October 21, 1954, Jack Kennedy underwent the first of two major operations. These were very risky because he suffered from Addison's disease, which interferes with anesthetics. Although he survived the operations, he caught an infection

But he did recover, and during the months of recuperation that followed, Jack was not idle. He decided to write a book about senators who had risked their jobs fighting for causes they believed in, against their constituents' wishes. The book, called *Profiles in Courage*, became a bestseller when it was published in 1956. It won the Pulitzer Prize for Biography

Despite the pain caused by his health problems, Jack pursued his career enthusiastically and remained popular with voters. On November 5, 1958, he was re-elected senator by a huge margin, winning the election with 73.6 percent of votes cast–the largest margin ever in the state of Massachusetts. He vowed he would run in the next election for the top political job in the United States: U.S. President.

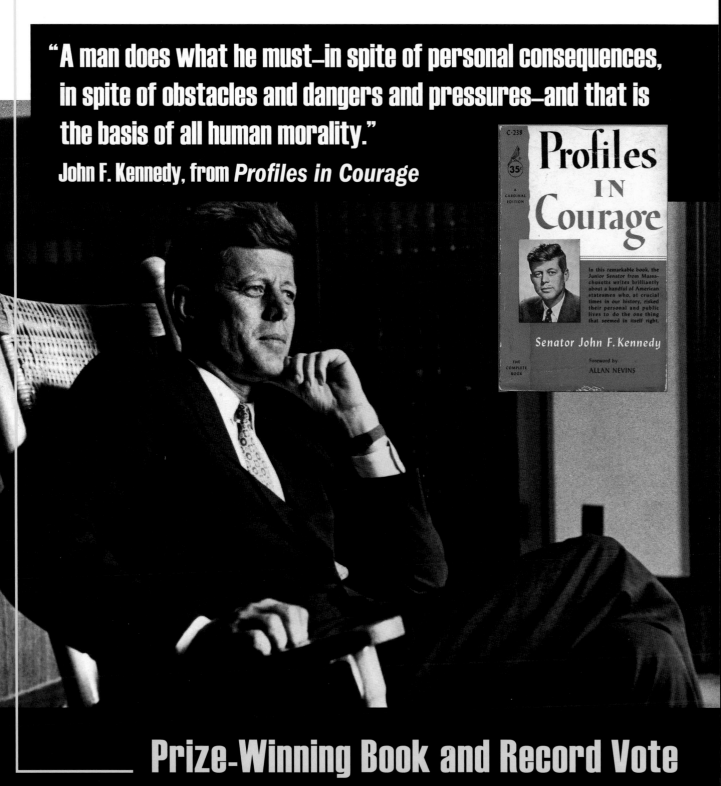

"A man does what he must–in spite of personal consequences, in spite of obstacles and dangers and pressures–and that is the basis of all human morality."

John F. Kennedy, from *Profiles in Courage*

C-238

Profiles
IN
Courage

In this remarkable book, the Junior Senator from Massachusetts writes brilliantly about a handful of American statesmen who, at crucial times in our history, risked their personal and public lives to do the one thing that seemed in itself right.

Senator John F. Kennedy

Foreword by
ALLAN NEVINS

Prize-Winning Book and Record Vote

Jack makes a coffee stop during his campaign to become the Democratic presidential candidate.

In January 1960, Jack Kennedy made an official announcement that he would run for President. But there was a lot of campaigning work to do first to win the nomination from the Democratic Party. Jack traveled all over the United States and worked very long hours telling people about his plans. His hard work paid off: on July 13, 1960, Jack was nominated to run for President. He asked Lyndon B. Johnson, a senator from Texas, to be his running mate and future Vice President. This was the moment Jack had been waiting for: a chance to really change the world for the better. When he won the nomination, Kennedy spoke of how America was on the edge of a "New Frontier," poised to tackle a set of challenges relating to human rights, peace, education, and space travel.

On September 26, 1960, John F. Kennedy faced Richard M. Nixon–the Republican candidate who was then vice president–in the first-ever televised presidential debate. Millions of viewers tuned in to hear what they had to say, so they could decide for themselves who would make the better leader.

But it was what they saw that mattered. Jack was calm and well-spoken, as well as young and handsome. The older Nixon appeared nervous and was visibly sweating. Many people believe that this debate swayed Americans to vote for Kennedy as the better choice.

The presidential candidates take part in the first-ever televised debate.

> "We stand today on the edge of a New Frontier... of unknown opportunities and perils..."
> from a JFK campaign speech, 1960

Presidential Candidate

John F. Kennedy swears the Oath of Office on January 20, 1961.

On November 8, 1960, election votes were being counted at polling stations across the United States. At around midnight, the *New York Times* announced that Senator John F. Kennedy had defeated Vice President Richard Nixon in the Presidential race. But he had won by just 0.01 percent, the smallest margin in generations. Some Republicans claimed the votes had been tampered with, but the count was honored.

It was a night to remember: at 43 years old, JFK (as people began calling him) was the youngest president ever to be elected, and also the first Catholic. One of the first things he did was to appoint his younger brother, Robert F. Kennedy, as U.S. Attorney General.

On January 20, 1961, John F. Kennedy was sworn into office as the 35th President of the United States. Huge crowds of people gathered outside the Capitol building in Washington D.C., in deep snow and freezing temperatures. Millions more watched the ceremony on TV. President Kennedy gave a heartfelt speech, urging Americans to join together with him to fight the "common enemies of man: tyranny, poverty, disease, and war itself."

That night, a lavish ball was held at the White House. Writers, artists, musicians, and film stars attended, including Frank Sinatra, Mahalia Jackson, Sidney Poitier, Nat King Cole, and Ella Fitzgerald. With a young, enthusiastic couple and their two small children in the White House, many felt that America had begun a new era of optimism. In years to come, the Kennedy administration would be nicknamed "Camelot," after the legendary and idyllic court of King Arthur in Great Britain.

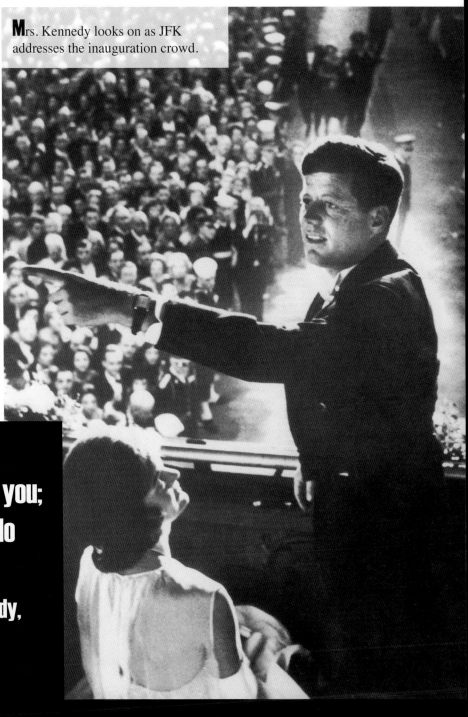

Mrs. Kennedy looks on as JFK addresses the inauguration crowd.

"Ask not what your country can do for you; ask what you can do for your country."
President John F. Kennedy, Inaugural Address, January 20, 1961

Election and Inauguration

Fidel Castro seized political power in Cuba in 1959.

Dr. FIDEL CASTRO

FIEL TELEVISION REVOLUCION

One of the first things President Kennedy did in his new job was to establish the Peace Corps on March 1, 1961. The Peace Corps offers hands-on help to developing countries, and is devoted to world peace and friendship. However, in 1961, the Cold War–a power struggle between the United States and the Soviet Union–had been in place since World War II ended in 1945. There was mistrust on both sides of the "Iron Curtain," a political border that had divided communist Soviet Bloc countries from the democratic West. The government of Cuba was run by a dictator named Fidel Castro, a Communist whose ideals clashed with American democracy. Castro also had close ties with Nikita Khrushchev, the leader of the Soviet Union. Because the island of Cuba lies so close to the U.S. off the coast of Florida, JFK wanted to overthrow Castro's regime and create a non-communist government there, removing the threat to American security.

On April 17, 1961, President Kennedy allowed a band of CIA-trained Cuban exiles to invade their own homeland. This secret invasion took place on three beaches bordering the Bahìa de Cochinos (Bay of Pigs) area of Cuba. But Castro had heard of the attack and had prepared his own armed forces, who had been trained in Soviet Bloc (communist) countries. Within three days, the Cuban exiles were defeated by Castro's forces. As a new President, this loss put JFK in a difficult position with his political opponents.

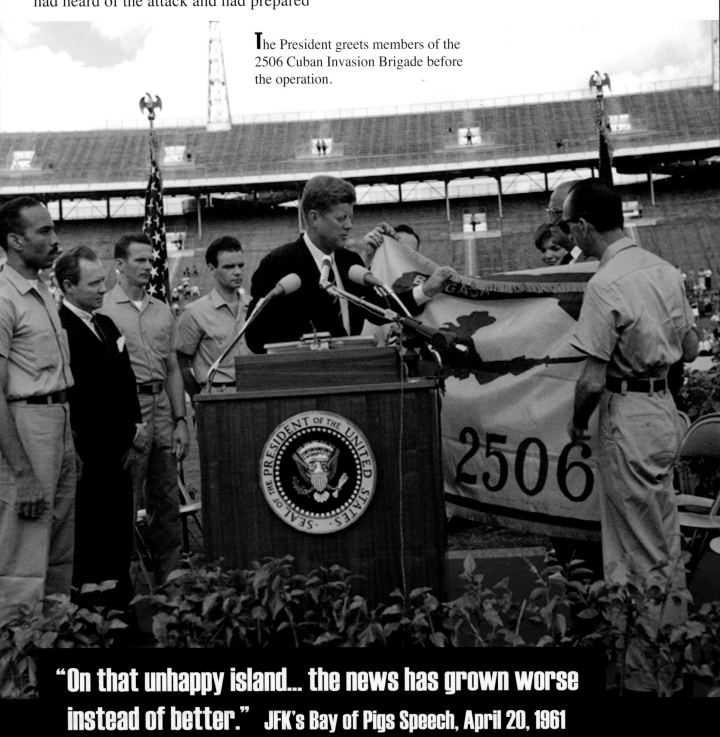

The President greets members of the 2506 Cuban Invasion Brigade before the operation.

"On that unhappy island... the news has grown worse instead of better." JFK's Bay of Pigs Speech, April 20, 1961

Alan Shepard awaits lift-off in May 1961.

The Bay of Pigs invasion had been the low point of JFK's career so far; privately, he'd been terribly upset about its failure. The President quickly turned his attention to another area of Cold War competition with the Soviet Union: the Space Race. The Soviets had already sent Yuri Gagarin into space on April 12, 1961, and the United States had some catching up to do to demonstrate its power to the world. On May 5, 1961, Alan Shepard stepped aboard the Freedom 7 spaceship to become the second man and the first American to travel in space. Millions of people were glued to their television screens as they watched the launch of the Project Mercury rocket from Cape Canaveral, Florida. Controlled by Shepard, the suborbital flight lasted just 15 minutes, and was a success. After a dramatic landing and recovery from the Atlantic Ocean, Shepard was hailed as a national hero and received honors from NASA.

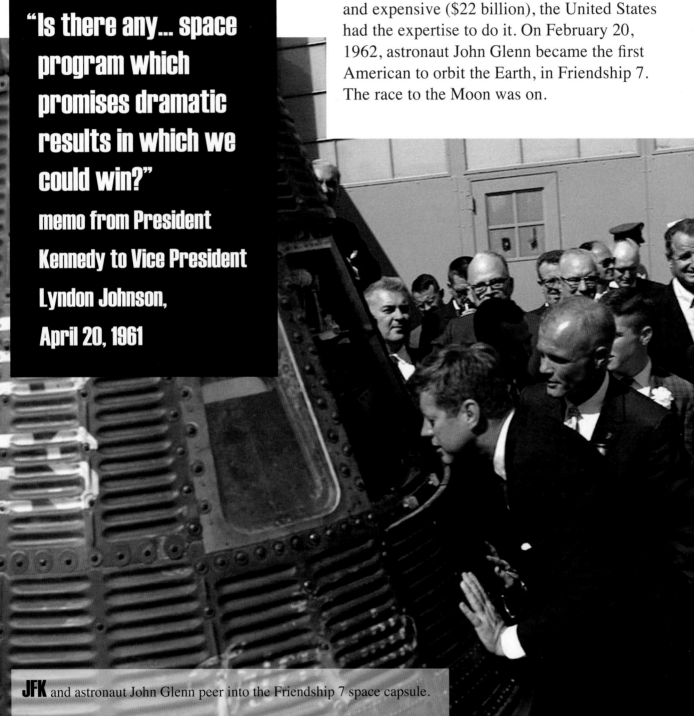

After consulting with Vice President Johnson, who had backed the space program since 1957, and NASA official James Webb, President Kennedy held a special session of Congress on May 25, 1961. By the end of the decade, Kennedy said, the nation would put a man on the Moon. While this would be both technically difficult and expensive ($22 billion), the United States had the expertise to do it. On February 20, 1962, astronaut John Glenn became the first American to orbit the Earth, in Friendship 7. The race to the Moon was on.

> "Is there any... space program which promises dramatic results in which we could win?"
>
> memo from President Kennedy to Vice President Lyndon Johnson, April 20, 1961

JFK and astronaut John Glenn peer into the Friendship 7 space capsule.

Space Race Begins

The building of the Berlin Wall, 1961.

When World War II ended, Germany had been divided into two zones: East Germany, ruled by the communist Soviet Union, and West Germany, a capitalist democracy like the United States. The city of Berlin was also divided. Millions of East Germans did not want to live in a communist country, so they moved to West Germany. But the Soviet government did not like this. President Kennedy met the Soviet leader Nikita Khrushchev in Vienna, Austria in June 1961, to talk about Berlin. The meeting was not a success: Khrushchev made threats, and the 'Cold War' between the United States and the Soviet Union worsened. Under Khrushchev's orders, construction of the Berlin Wall began on Aug 13, 1961. It ran across canals, through cemeteries, and along streets. People were no longer free to move between East and West Berlin. The wall was heavily guarded—anyone who tried to climb over was shot.

Shortly after the Berlin Wall was built, President Kennedy worried that South Vietnam would also become communist. On November 22, 1961, he approved the sending of 1,000 U.S. military advisors to South Vietnam to try to stop corruption in its government, led by Ngo Dinh Diem.

Later, on December 15, 1961, President Kennedy renewed America's commitment to help Vietnam stay independent. But these moves only increased U.S. involvement in Vietnam, which would soon escalate into a very unpopular war.

"It is an unfortunate fact that we can secure peace only by preparing for war." John F. Kennedy

A meeting between JFK and Nguyen Dinh Thuan, Vietnamese Secretary of State, took place in June, 1961.

Berlin Wall and Roots of the Vietnam War

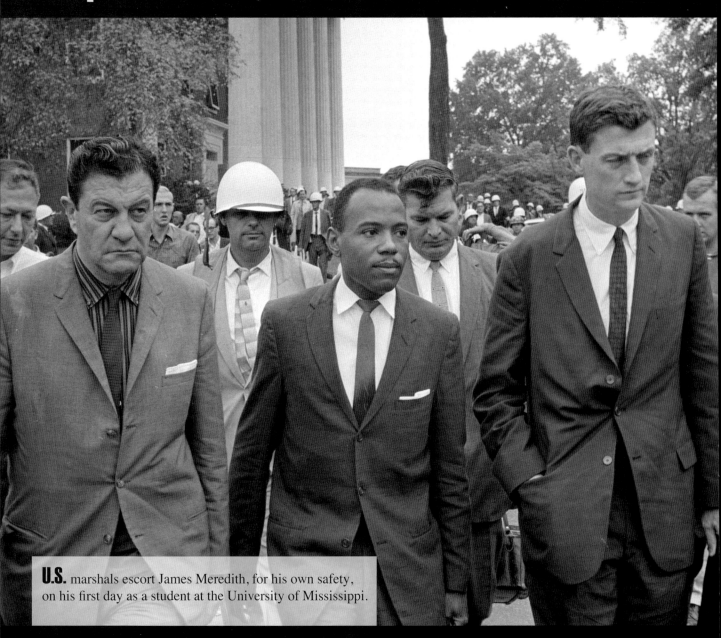

U.S. marshals escort James Meredith, for his own safety, on his first day as a student at the University of Mississippi.

The United States Constitution says that all men are created equal. But in the early 1960s, not all Americans were treated equally. There was a lot of prejudice against African Americans, especially in the Deep South, where attitudes left over from the days of slavery–abolished a hundred years earlier–still lingered. Many people still thought that segregation in areas such as education–where black and white students attended separate schools–was acceptable.

On September 30, 1962, a young man named James Meredith went to register at the University of Mississippi, the same as hundreds of other students that day. But James Meredith was an African American, and he happened to be the first African American to enroll at this all-white university.

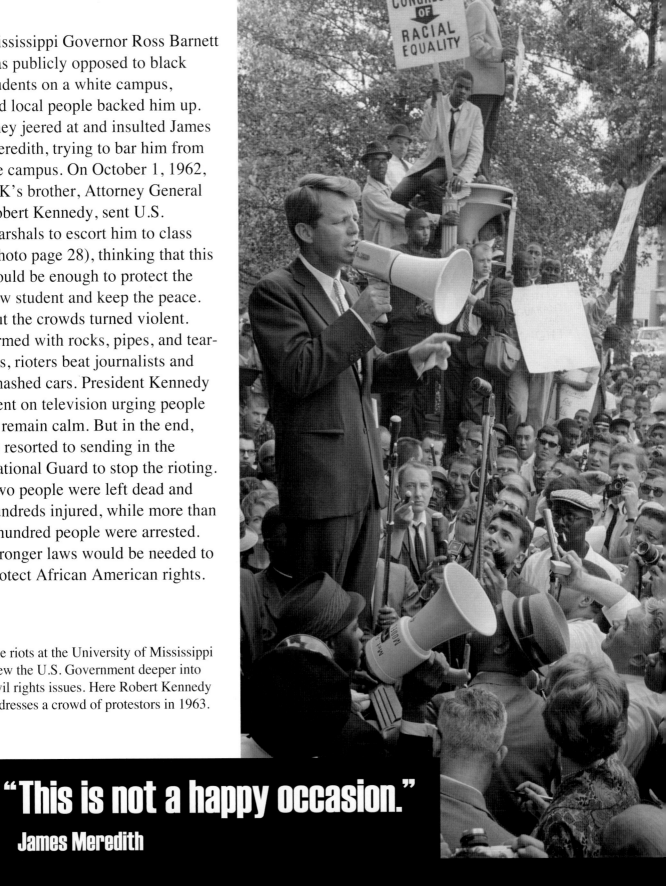

Mississippi Governor Ross Barnett was publicly opposed to black students on a white campus, and local people backed him up. They jeered at and insulted James Meredith, trying to bar him from the campus. On October 1, 1962, JFK's brother, Attorney General Robert Kennedy, sent U.S. Marshals to escort him to class (photo page 28), thinking that this would be enough to protect the new student and keep the peace. But the crowds turned violent. Armed with rocks, pipes, and tear-gas, rioters beat journalists and smashed cars. President Kennedy went on television urging people to remain calm. But in the end, he resorted to sending in the National Guard to stop the rioting. Two people were left dead and hundreds injured, while more than a hundred people were arrested. Stronger laws would be needed to protect African American rights.

The riots at the University of Mississippi drew the U.S. Government deeper into civil rights issues. Here Robert Kennedy addresses a crowd of protestors in 1963.

"This is not a happy occasion."
James Meredith

University of Mississippi Riots

October 16-28, 1962

This labeled U.S. aerial photo shows a missile base under construction in Cuba.

LAUNCH POSITION

MISSILE-READY TENTS

MISSILE ERECTORS

After the Bay of Pigs invasion and the construction of the Berlin Wall, relations between the United States and Soviet Union became even more strained. The Cold War –which up until now had been contained to a few incidents–threatened to turn into full-blown combat. President Kennedy discovered from U.S. spy planes that the Soviets were installing nuclear weapons at their base in Cuba, making it much easier for the Soviets to launch a nuclear attack on the United States. Once begun, a nuclear war would have devastating effects on the entire planet. So on October 16, 1962, the President issued a quarantine that banned all offensive weapons from entering Cuba. U.S. Navy boats patrolled waters around the island to stop any suspicious foreign ships.

The Soviet Union realized the U.S. was serious about the ban. So on October 26, 1962, it backed down, promising to remove its missiles already installed in Cuba–if the U.S. agreed not to invade Cuba again and also removed its nuclear weapons from Turkey. The Cuban Missile Crisis had been averted. But the call had been a very close one. The crisis led to legislation for the Test Ban Agreement of 1963. This stated that it was vital for nuclear weapons to be banned from both sides of the Cold War. The arms race between the Soviet Union and the United States would have to slow down to save the world from certain destruction.

President Kennedy makes a televised speech about the Cuban Missile Crisis on October 22, 1962.

"It was the most dangerous moment in human history."

Arthur Schlesinger, Jr., JFK aide and historian

The Cuban Missile Crisis

President Kennedy speaks to the nation about civil rights, June 1963.

President Kennedy now faced a growing moral crisis at home: racial discrimination. Many people were joining together to protest peacefully about continuing racial injustice towards African Americans. Worried that these protests would only act to anger people, the President and Robert Kennedy decided that the best way to ensure equality was to enforce civil rights through a new, stronger law.

On June 11, 1963, President Kennedy proposed a bill to Congress to strengthen the enforcement of voting and other rights for African Americans and help end racism. But just hours after the address, civil rights leader Medgar Evers was assassinated. His murder served to strengthen the President's resolve to support the civil rights cause even further.

One of the country's most famous civil rights activists, Dr. Martin Luther King, Jr., organized a march in Washington D.C. with his colleagues, to raise awareness of African Americans' plight. Dr. King was clear that peaceful protest and not violence was the best way to conquer prejudice and achieve the aim of racial equality. On the morning of August 28, 1963, a huge crowd of 250,000 people attended the march–people of all races, classes, and religions.

They gathered around the Lincoln Memorial to listen to the speakers' words. Silence fell upon the crowd as Martin Luther King, Jr. delivered one of the most moving speeches of all time. In his "I Have a Dream" speech, he hoped that one day his children would be judged not by the color of their skin but by the content of their character. Impressed with King's speech, JFK promised he would advance civil rights reforms within the government.

Martin Luther King, Jr. addresses a huge crowd of more than 250,000 people gathered around the Lincoln Memorial on August 28, 1963.

Civil Rights Act and Martin Luther King, Jr.

The Kennedys, just moments before JFK's assassination

On November 22, 1963, U.S. President John F. Kennedy and his wife, Jackie, arrived by plane in Dallas, Texas, to give some political speeches. The day began well: they shook hands with well-wishers, then set off on a motorcade tour of the city. Thousands of excited people lined the streets to catch a glimpse of the First Couple in the back seat of an open limousine. Then, at 12:30 PM, just as President Kennedy raised his hand to wave, the car was sprayed with bullets from what sounded like a rifle. Hit in the neck and head, he slumped towards his horrified wife, who tried to hold him up.

Secret servicemen drew guns as the driver quickly drove the limo away, while crowds looked on with dread. The President was raced to Parkland Memorial Hospital where surgeons tried to operate, but at 1:00 PM John F. Kennedy was pronounced dead.

At 2:38 PM, on board Air Force One, Vice President Lyndon B. Johnson was sworn in as the 36th President of the United States. The brief ceremony was witnessed by Mrs. Johnson, Mrs. Kennedy, and a handful of government aides, all crammed into the small cabin.

Also on board was the President's body, which was flown back to Washington, D.C. and taken to a mortuary. Throughout the day's ordeal, Jackie Kennedy refused to leave her husband's body, also refusing to change her blood-stained clothes. She was heard to say: "I want them to see what they've done to Jack." The major U.S. television networks— CBS, NBC and ABC–suspended normal programming, and for the next three days they broadcast events as they unfolded. The world was in shock: one of America's most popular presidents had been assassinated.

"This is terrible– I cannot find words."
U.S. Senator Mike Mansfield

For the sake of national security, Lyndon B. Johnson was sworn in as U.S. President just hours after President Kennedy's assassination.

The Assassination of JFK

The coffin containing President Kennedy's body lies in state in the White House.

On November 23, 1963 at 4:30 AM, President Kennedy's body was moved to the East Room of the White House where he remained for 24 hours. This was the same room where President Abraham Lincoln had lain after his assassination a hundred years earlier. Family members and friends said a private goodbye, while a vigil was kept by an honor guard and two Catholic priests.

The next day, the President's coffin was moved by horse-drawn wagon to the Rotunda of the U.S. Capitol Building to lie in state. Jackie Kennedy knelt with her daughter Caroline, as she kissed the flag-covered coffin and said goodbye to her husband. Later, 250,000 people walked past the guarded coffin, all through the day and night, to pay their last respects.

The new president, Lyndon B. Johnson, declared Monday, November 25, 1963 a national day of mourning. The whole country stopped work as they watched the state funeral on television, many overwhelmed by tears. Mrs. Kennedy and her brothers-in-law led the funeral procession to St. Matthew's Cathedral, walking past a million people who lined the streets of Washington, D.C. The Kennedy children, Caroline and John Jr., met their mother at the cathedral to attend the Catholic funeral mass for their father.

While America mourned its youngest president ever to die in office, around 220 dignitaries from 90 countries–kings, queens, and premiers–came to pay their respects to one of the best-loved leaders of the 20th century. John F. Kennedy was laid to rest in Arlington National Cemetery. The world had changed forever.

J ackie Kennedy and her daughter, Caroline, say goodbye at JFK's funeral.

"We are saddened; we are stunned; we are perplexed."
Earl Warren, U.S. Chief Justice

Aftermath and Funeral

Lee Harvey Oswald in police custody.

"They've taken me in because of the fact that I lived in the Soviet Union. I'm just a patsy!"

Lee Harvey Oswald

Forty minutes after President Kennedy was shot, Lee Harvey Oswald was arrested for the murder of police officer J.D. Tippit on a street in Dallas. Oswald, a 24-year-old former U.S. Marine, was a highly-trained marksman who had lived in the Soviet Union and supported communist ideas. Shortly after he ducked into a movie theatre, police stormed in. Oswald was heard to say, "Well, it's all over now." He tried to shoot an officer but his gun failed to fire. Police charged him with Tippit's murder and also with the assassination of the President. Oswald denied that he had any involvement in either shooting, but the authorities were sure they had got their man.

But Oswald was not to stand trial for the charges in court. On November 24, 1963, as he was being transferred to another prison, a nightclub owner named Jack Ruby pushed his way through reporters and fired a gun at close range at Lee Harvey Oswald. Millions looked on in disbelief as television cameras broadcast the grisly moment live on screen. Two hours later, Oswald died at the same hospital where the President had died the day before. Because Oswald was never tried, U.S. government committees were set up to decide who had killed the President. In 1964, the Warren Commission concluded that Lee Harvey Oswald had fired the fatal rifle shots, and that he had worked alone. But as the years passed, many people came to believe there had been a conspiracy to kill JFK.

Nightclub owner Jack Ruby shoots Lee Harvey Oswald on live television.

Lee Harvey Oswald–Assassin?

Martin Luther King, Jr. and Robert Kennedy (center) with civil rights leaders and President Johnson.

After JFK's death, both Dr. Martin Luther King, Jr. and Robert Kennedy carried on the civil rights work of the Kennedy administration. Sadly, Martin Luther King, Jr. started receiving death threats. On April 3, 1968, in Memphis, Tennessee, King delivered his famous "I have been to the mountaintop" speech. In it, he said he had done his life's work and was ready for whatever might happen. The following night, April 4, 1968, Martin Luther King, Jr. was chatting with colleague Jesse Jackson on a hotel balcony in Memphis. At 6:01 PM a shot rang out and King was hit in the head. He was raced to the hospital, but at 7 PM, Martin Luther King, Jr. was pronounced dead. When the news was broadcast, riots broke out in cities across America. Two months later, James Earl Ray was arrested for suspected murder and later convicted for the assassination of Dr. King.

As JFK's Attorney General, Robert Kennedy had played a large part in crucial decision-making and was well-respected. So in the spring of 1968, when Senator Kennedy campaigned to become the Democratic presidential candidate, there was another chance for a young, optimistic man to lead the nation. Spirits were high; Arthur Schlesinger, Jr. called it "an uproarious campaign, filled with enthusiasm and fun."

But just as Robert Kennedy looked set to win the nomination, tragedy struck once more. On June 5, 1968, just after midnight, Robert Kennedy was fatally shot at the Ambassador Hotel in Los Angeles, California. A Jordanian Palestinian immigrant named Sirhan Sirhan was convicted of the crime. As with JFK, many people believe the assassinations of both Martin Luther King, Jr. and Robert Kennedy were the result of conspiracies.

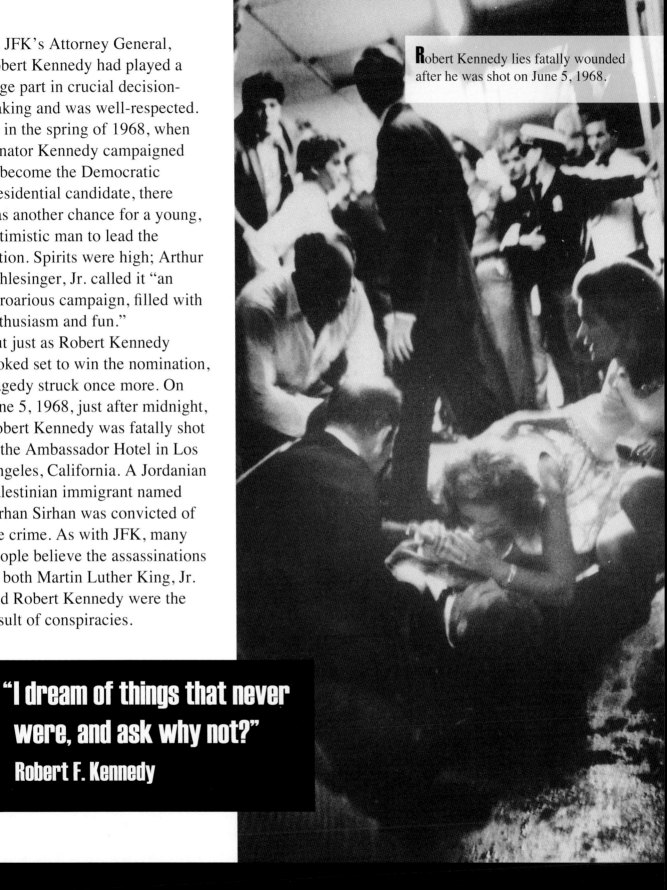

Robert Kennedy lies fatally wounded after he was shot on June 5, 1968.

"I dream of things that never were, and ask why not?"
Robert F. Kennedy

Assassinations of MLK and RFK

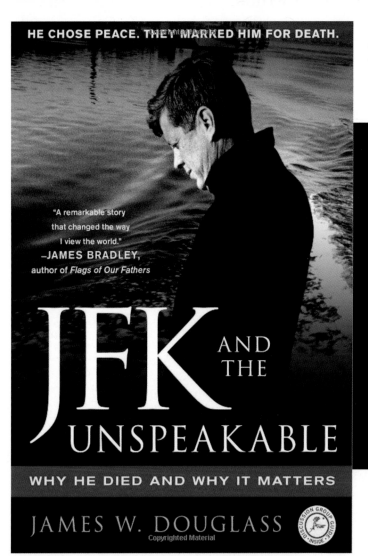

HE CHOSE PEACE. THEY MARKED HIM FOR DEATH.

"A remarkable story that changed the way I view the world."
—JAMES BRADLEY, author of *Flags of Our Fathers*

JFK AND THE UNSPEAKABLE

WHY HE DIED AND WHY IT MATTERS

JAMES W. DOUGLASS
Copyrighted Material

A conspiracy or not? Authors and film directors continue to debate this issue.

> ## "I'll tell you something about Kennedy's murder that will rock you...Kennedy was trying to get Castro, but Castro got to him first."
>
> ### Lyndon B. Johnson, quoted in a confidential interview to journalist Howard K. Smith

Since 1963, people have conjectured who was really behind the assassination of President Kennedy. Was Lee Harvey Oswald the killer, and did he act alone out of a personal hatred for JFK or America (the "lone gunman theory")? Or did Oswald act as an agent on behalf of the Soviet Union or the Cuban government, both of whom had reason to want JFK dead? Was the Mafia behind the killing or–more disturbingly–was the CIA involved in a conspiracy? As people delve deeper into the mystery, new evidence emerges each year: documents, audio tapes, eyewitness accounts. Over 1,000 books have been written that explore the conspiracy theories. Many have become best-sellers, illustrating people's endless fascination. In 1991, director Oliver Stone made the controversial film *JFK* about an alleged cover-up within the U.S. government.

Today President Kennedy is remembered as a dynamic and charismatic leader who brought positive change to America during his thousand days in office. His work with civil rights has improved life for millions, as have organizations he founded to help disadvantaged people, such as the Peace Corps and the Committee for People with Intellectual Disabilities. The President and Mrs. Kennedy's love of the arts led to the creation of the Kennedy Center, a national leader in arts and music education. Perhaps the most dramatic fruition of JFK's legacy came on July 20, 1969, when three Apollo 11 astronauts took the first human steps on the surface of the Moon.

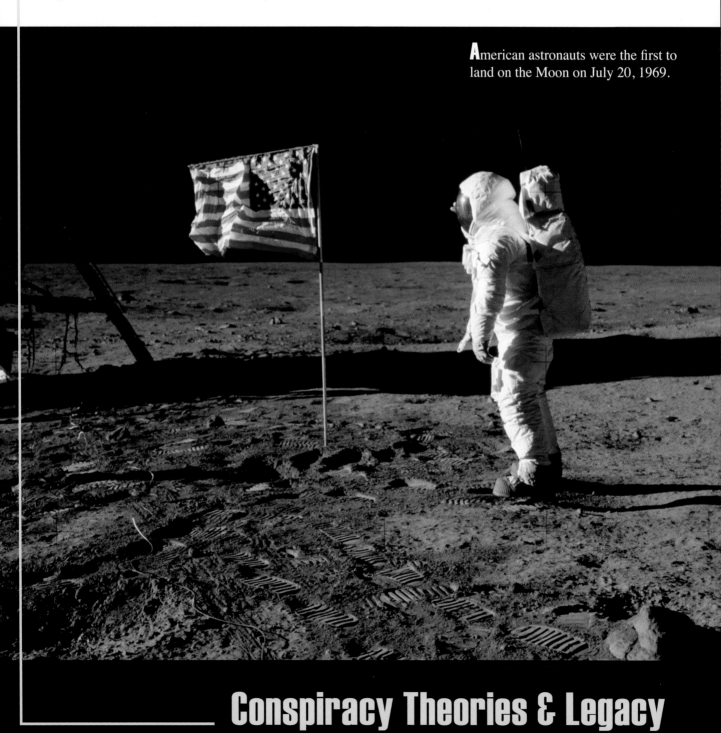

American astronauts were the first to land on the Moon on July 20, 1969.

Conspiracy Theories & Legacy

Senator Edward Kennedy, pictured before his death in 2009

The life of John F. Kennedy has been an inspiration for many people, including future leaders of the United States. As well as inspiring his brother Robert Kennedy, another younger brother–Edward "Ted" Kennedy– campaigned for the presidential nomination in 1980. He did not win, but went on to become the third longest-serving senator in American history (1962–2009), also acting as chairman on several Senate committees. Edward Kennedy's career was full of remarkable achievements as he worked to improve civil rights, education, healthcare and the minimum wage. The "Lion of the Senate" remained in office until his death in 2009.

But JFK's reach went beyond the family circle. In 1963, 16-year-old Bill Clinton met President Kennedy at the White House Rose Garden. In a photo that captured that moment, Clinton's admiration for JFK is clear. He claims it was a defining moment in his life, and in 1992, Bill Clinton was elected the 42nd President of the United States. In 2008, Barack Obama became the first African American to be elected U.S. President. He has also acknowledged his admiration for Kennedy's work. Comparisons have been made between the two leaders, even by JFK's daughter Caroline Bouvier Kennedy. An attorney and author, Caroline campaigned for Obama's election and his re-election in 2012.

In 1963, Jackie Kennedy lit an eternal flame at the grave of John F. Kennedy. His flame still burns brightly today.

Barack Obama has declared his respect for JFK's work.

"We cannot forget we are heirs of this president who showed us what is possible."
President Barack Obama on JFK

Inspiring Future Generations

Glossary

Air Force One The aircraft that transports the President of the United States on official journeys.

Addison's disease A disease that affects the adrenal glands.

administration A period when a particular president is in office and the officials in the executive branch of government work under him.

assassination The murder of a political leader, activist, or other important person.

CIA (Central Intelligence Agency) The U.S. Government organization that collects data on foreign affairs and people.

civil rights The rights of each person in a society to equality, regardless of race or gender, and to the right to vote.

Cold War A dangerous, unfriendly situation between two countries, with the threat of war breaking out. The U.S. and Soviet Union had a Cold War from 1945–1991.

communism An economic system where everyone owns property equally, and no one profits from another's work.

Congress The legislative (law-making) branch of the U.S. Government consisting of the Senate and the House of Representatives.

congressman A member of the House of Representatives.

conspiracy A secret plot made up by two or more people to do something illegal.

constituents Citizens who are represented by an elected government official.

democracy A country where people elect representatives to speak on their behalf.

Democrat A member of the Democratic Political Party.

dictator A ruler with total power over a country, and who has often seized power by force.

Eastern Bloc Former communist states of Eastern Europe that were ruled by the Soviet Union.

eternal flame A small fire that is kept burning in remembrance of someone who has died.

First Lady The wife of the President of the United States.

House of Representatives Part of the U.S. Congress, with a number of elected representatives from each U.S. state in proportion to the size of its population.

humanitarian Someone who is involved in improving people's lives.

Iron Curtain The military and political border dividing Europe into two separate areas, from 1945 to 1991.

Marshal A type of U.S. law-enforcement officer.

motorcade A group of vehicles traveling together.

NASA (National Aeronautics and Space Administration) The U.S. Government organization set up to plan space travel and research.

nomination When a political candidate is chosen by their party to represent them.

nuclear weapons Weapons where an atom is divided to release energy and cause a highly destructive explosion.

polling station A place where people go to vote during an election.

presidential election Held every four years, the election for U.S. President follows a long political process.

Republican A member of the Republican Political Party.

segregation When one group of people is separated from another because of race, religion or other differences.

Senate Part of the U.S. Congress whose members have the most power to make laws in the government.

senator A member of the U.S. Senate. There are two senators from each state, regardless of size.

Space Race The competition between the United States and Soviet Union for space exploration in the 1960s.

union An organization that helps protect the rights of a group of workers.

U.S. Constitution A document that sets out the rules and laws of the U.S. Government.

Warren Commission Government body set up to investigate the assassination of JFK.

http://www.whitehouse.gov/about/presidents
Discover fascinating facts about John F. Kennedy and all the presidents
on the official White House website.

http://www.jfklibrary.org
Excellent source of information on the life of John F. Kennedy and the
whole Kennedy family. With biographies, photos, videos, key speeches,
maps and more.

http://www.presidentialtimeline.org
Interactive timelines on the presidency of JFK and other presidents,
with zoomable photos and text. Also includes a special exhibit on the
Peace Corps.

http://www.cr.nps.gov/nr/twhp/wwwlps/lessons/33jfk/33jfk.htm
Learn about the birthplace of JFK and the neighborhood where
he grew up.

http://millercenter.org/president/speeches
Search for and read transcripts from President John F. Kennedy's
speeches.

Note to parents and teachers

Every effort has been made by the Publishers to ensure that the websites in this
book are suitable for children, that they are of the highest educational value, and
that they contain no inappropriate or offensive material. However, because of
the nature of the Internet, it is impossible to guarantee that the contents of these
sites will not be altered. We strongly advise that Internet access is supervised by
a responsible adult.